Robin Spie g

The Holiday Collection

Photography by Larry Kosson
Deja View Photography,Inc.
dejaviewphotography.com

Piano transcriptions by Dennis Desormier
musicatechnica.com
edited by Robin Spielberg & Dennis Desormier

ISBN 0-9705633-2-9

Spobs Music Inc

for a complete listing of Robin Spielberg's songbooks, please visit www.robinspielberg.com

TABLE OF CONTENTS

all songs arranged by Robin Spielberg
**indicates original composition by Robin Spielberg All music published by Spobs Music Inc. (ASCAP) P.O. Box 43158; Upper Montclair, NJ 07043*

A Change of Season

by Robin Spielberg

Recorded by Robin Spielberg on the album *In the Heart of Winter* (North Star Records NS0075)

mp
f

mp
5
5
5
5
1 5

f
1 5
8va
p
(8va)

(8va)
(8va)
(8va)
(8va)
(8va)

(8va)
5

(8va)
(8va)
(8va)
(8va)
loco
pp
Ped.
6
mp
Ped.

Angels We Have Heard on High

Traditional French carol
arranged by Robin Spielberg

Recorded by Robin Spielberg on the album *The Christmas Collection* (playMountain Music PMM104)

8va
mf
pedal as in the beginning
8vb

Interlude
8va
8vb
(8va)
mp
8va
8va
(8va)
5 1
8va
8va

Verse
mf
f
8vb

ff
8vb

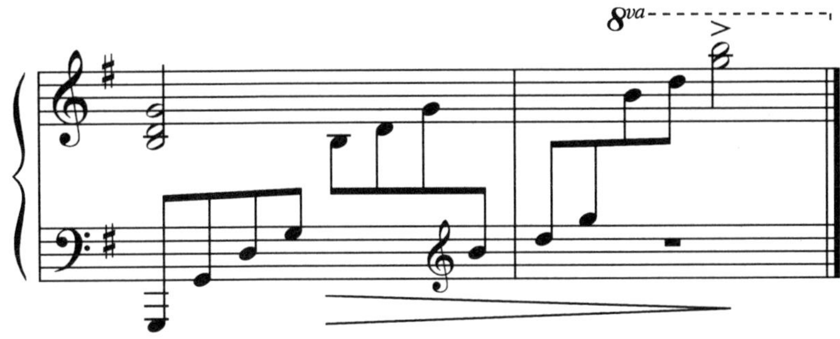
8va

Jingle Bells

Traditional
arranged by Robin Spielberg

Recorded by Robin Spielberg on the album *The Christmas Collection* (playMountain Music PMM104)

Jingle Bells

(R.H.)

f
ff

1 5
8va
mp
(8va)
(8va)
rit.
at tempo
loco
rit.
8vb

First Night

by Robin Spielberg

Recorded by Robin Spielberg on the album *American Chanukah* (playMountain Music PMM103)
and on the album *In the Heart of Winter* (North Star Music NS0075)

mf
8vb
1 5
mf
at tempo

8va
rit.
p
at tempo
(8va)
mp
rit.
mf
at tempo

f
Slower, with rubato.
rit.
8va
pp
(8va)
loco

It Came Upon a Midnight Clear

by Richard S. Willis
arranged by Robin Spielberg

Recorded by Robin Spielberg on the album *The Christmas Collection* (playMountain Music PMM104)

mf
1 5
rit.
at tempo

It came upon a midnight clear

It came upon a midnight clear

Coda
pp
rit.

Hark! The Herald Angels Sing

by Felix Mendelssohn & Chas. Wesley
arranged by Robin Spielberg

Recorded by Robin Spielberg on the LunaMoon album *Spirits of the Holiday* (North Star Records NS0066)

rit.
Interlude
mp
mf
rit.
mf
at tempo
8vb
8vb

rit.
Verse: Majestically
mf
at tempo
rit.
p
8vb
mp
at tempo

molto rit.
mp
at tempo
f
mf
rit.
mp
8vb

Chanukah, Chanukah/I Have a Little Dreydel

Traditional
arranged by Robin Spielberg

Recorded by Robin Spielberg on the album *American Chanukah* (playMountain Music PMM104)

Ped.
Interlude
mf
8va
(8va)
mp

"Chanukah, Chanukah"
ff
mf

Interlude
8va
loco
8va
"I Have a Little Dreydel"
(8va)
p

(8va)
mp
f
mf
Interlude
mp
8va

(8va)

f
p

Coda: "I Have a Little Dreydel"
8va

(8va)
"Chanukah, Chanukah"
rit.
8va

Carol of the Bells

Traditional
arranged by Robin Spielberg

Recorded by Robin Spielberg on the album *The Christmas Collection* (playMountain Music PMM104)

1 5
1 5
1 5
Interlude
8va
1 5

(8va)
loco
ppp
Verse
mp
mf

mf
Interlude
mp
8va
7
mf

p
mf
pp
ppp
Verse
mf

Coda
8va
p
(8va)

(8va)
7
(8va)
loco
8va

In the Heart of Winter

by Robin Spielberg

Recorded by Robin Spielberg on the album *In the Heart of Winter* (North Star Music NS0075)

(8va)
(8va)
(8va)
6
rit.
In relief
8va
loco
Main Theme: Much more calmly and slowly with rubato

Poetic
5 2 1 1 1
5 2 1 1 1
sim.
8va

8va
More Briskly
8va
(8va)
(8va)
loco
8va

8va
8va
(8va)
(8va)
8va
(8va)
8va
8va

Original Tempo
8va
(8va)
6
1 2 5 4 2 1 2

In the Heart of Winter
by Robin Spielberg

In the heart of the winter
With snow all around
There's a kindness warm and gentle
Buried in the ground
You can hear her if you listen
Breathing quiet in her sleep
When she awakens you will see
All the secrets that she keeps
In the heart of the winter
In the heart of the winter.

Rock of Ages (Ma'oz Tzur)

Traditional
arranged by Robin Spielberg

Recorded by Robin Spielberg on the album *American Chanukah* (playMountain Music PMM103)

Rock of Ages (Ma'oz Tzur)

Interlude: *Gently*
rit.
at tempo
Verse: *as in prayer*
p
mf

mf
mf
Slower
mp
rit.
Coda
mf
at tempo
rit.

The Coventry Carol

Traditional
arranged by Robin Spielberg

Recorded by Robin Spielberg on the album *The Christmas Collection* (playMountain Music PMM104)

8va
mp
8va
mf
Interlude
8va
mp

(8va)
(8va)
(8va)
Verse
mf
mf

p

rit.
8va

In the Bleak Midwinter

Traditional
arranged by Robin Spielberg

Recorded by Robin Spielberg on the album *The Christmas Collection* (playMountain Music PMM104)

8va
at tempo
5 2 1 4 3 1 2 3
1 5
5 2 1 3 2 1
8va
1 5
Interlude
8va

8va
loco
rit.
Verse
at tempo
8va

8va
ppp
(8va)
mp
8va

Coda
8va
mf
8va
pp
1 5
(8va)
mp
8va
pp
8va

Zum Gali Gali

Traditional
arranged by Robin Spielberg

Recorded by Robin Spielberg on the album *American Chanukah* (playMountain Music PMM103)

p
mf
pp
ppp
mp
mp
pp
mp
8va
pp
mp

rit.
at tempo
pp
mf
pp
mf
8va
pp
mp
(8va)

Zum Gali Gali

This song was sung by the early Zionist pioneers before the founding of Israel. Many early Zionist pioneers settled in Galilee, and in Yiddish "To Gaililee" translates as "Zu dem Galil." It is plausible to think that the repeated words "Zum Gali Gali" are not nonsense syllables as many believe, but rather a "folk Yiddish" pronunciation of "To Gaililee." The second half of the song is in Hebrew:

Hechalutz le'man avodah;
Avodah le'man hechalutz.
Hashalom le'man ha'amin;
Ha'amin le'man hashalom.

This translates to "Pioneers all work as one; all work as pioneers. Peace be for the world; the world shall be for peace." It has been suggested that since the early Zionists were unsure whether their national language should be Yiddish or Hebrew, the song's lyrics were written in both.

Silent Night

composed by Franz Gruber
arranged by Robin Spielberg

Recorded by Robin Spielberg on the album *The Christmas Collection* (playMountain Music PMM104)

at tempo
mf
8vb
8vb
8vb
8vb

Interlude
rit.
at tempo
8vb
Verse: Majestically
rit.
f
at tempo
8vb
8vb

mf
8vb
f
rit.
8vb
at tempo
8vb
Coda: Gently
mp
rit.
8vb

ROBIN SPIELBERG

Few pianists can speak the language of music as fluently, eloquently and beautifully as Robin Spielberg. Mesmerizing audiences with inspired tales, extraordinary piano technique and heartfelt performances, Ms. Spielberg is in the top echelon of contemporary composer/pianists.

*Following graduation from New York University, Robin began her performance career in New York City's finest piano rooms. Enthralling audiences with her arrangements of classics and enchanting them with her original compositions, Robin quickly gained a loyal following. In 1993 Robin recorded her first CD, **Heal of the Hand**. She was named to the prestigious Steinway Artist Roster in 1996 and made her Carnegie Hall concert debut in 1997. Robin keeps an active touring schedule, entertaining thousands of people throughout the country each year. Robin's music has been featured on **CBS Saturday Morning, LifeTime Live, ABC News** and **National Public Radio.** Robin Spielberg is the Celebrity Spokesperson for The American Music Therapy Association (AMTA).*

*As of this writing, Robin Spielberg has recorded twelve albums, including three collections of original piano solos (**Heal of the Hand, Songs of the Spirit, Dreaming of Summer**), four recordings for the holidays (**Spirit of the Holidays, In the Heart of Winter, American Chanukah, The Christmas Collection**), two recordings of American standards and film songs (**Unchained Melodies, With A Song in My Heart**), a recording of original compositions for piano/ensemble (**In the Arms of the Wind**), a collaborative CD containing instrumentals, lullabies and sung ballads celebrating mothers and motherhood (**Mother**), and **Beautiful Dreamer**, lullabies for the parent & child on solo piano. **The Holiday Collection** is the artist's fourth solo piano folio.*

Robin Spielberg & her husband Larry Kosson reside in New Jersey where they manage SMG Artists, an artist booking agency, playMountain Music, an independent record label, Spobs Music Publishing, and Deja View Inc., a commercial photography studio. They have one daughter.

Robin Spielberg's web site contains information on all of her recordings, and songbooks. It also contains photos, her current concert schedule, reviews and audio samples. It is located at www.robinspielberg.com